AF151810

YOUR KNOWLEDGE HAS VALUE

- We will publish your bachelor's and master's thesis, essays and papers

- Your own eBook and book - sold worldwide in all relevant shops

- Earn money with each sale

Upload your text at www.GRIN.com
and publish for free

Marcus Gießmann

What Meaning do the Dead have in James Joyce´s "The Dead"?

GRIN Verlag

Bibliografische Information der Deutschen Nationalbibliothek:

Die Deutsche Bibliothek verzeichnet diese Publikation in der Deutschen National-
bibliografie; detaillierte bibliografische Daten sind im Internet über http://dnb.d-
nb.de/ abrufbar.

Imprint:

Copyright © 2013 GRIN Verlag GmbH
Druck und Bindung: Books on Demand GmbH, Norderstedt Germany
ISBN: 978-3-656-49956-5

This book at GRIN:

http://www.grin.com/en/e-book/233033/what-meaning-do-the-dead-have-in-james-
joyce-s-the-dead

GRIN - Your knowledge has value

Der GRIN Verlag publiziert seit 1998 wissenschaftliche Arbeiten von Studenten, Hochschullehrern und anderen Akademikern als eBook und gedrucktes Buch. Die Verlagswebsite www.grin.com ist die ideale Plattform zur Veröffentlichung von Hausarbeiten, Abschlussarbeiten, wissenschaftlichen Aufsätzen, Dissertationen und Fachbüchern.

Visit us on the internet:

http://www.grin.com/

http://www.facebook.com/grincom

http://www.twitter.com/grin_com

Friedrich-Alexander-Universität Erlangen-Nürnberg
Sprachenzentrum

What Meaning do the Dead have in James Joyce´s *The Dead*?

Term Paper – Arts and Humanities

Author: Marcus Gießmann

Date: August 12th 2013

Content

1. Structure

Before, while and after reading *The Dead* by James Joyce one question seems omnipresent – not least because of the title: What connection does the narrative have to the dead? This question yields another one, namely "What does that mean?"

In order to approach these two questions appropriately and to reach epistemically satisfying conclusions, I propose a simple structure which allows us to consider the issues in question. Firstly, we will look at three elements of the storyline: The environment, the people and most importantly Gabriel. Each element will be investigated concerning its role and meaning for the whole story and as to how appropriate connections between elements could be drawn. Following this, we will be able to rank the elements in regards to their importance with reference to the answers to our initial questions. Obviously Gabriel is the most important element and hence will help us best to deliver answers to our questions. Therefore we must take a closer look at him.

I will argue that Gabriel is the key element in answering the first of our initial questions. The whole narrative culminates in the end, when Gabriel realized that he was only a substitute for the deceased Michael Furey – the early love of his wife Gretta, if not the love of her life.[1]

The answer to the second question is that the special circumstances which generate a paradoxical[2] connection are nothing more than the inflexible and rigid attitudes of people who interact with their surroundings and cause them to be rigid and uniform.

2. *The Dead*

2.1 Background of *The Dead*

The Dead was written in spring 1907 and is the last of 15 stories making up *Dubliners*. *Dubliners* is a collection of short stories, which were written between 1904-1907 and reflect on four main topics, i.e. childhood, adolescence, maturity and public life.[3] In contrast to the other stories in *Dubliners*, *The Dead* could function as an epilogue because it combines the

---

[1] See Joyce, 1914, pp. 2197-2197 lines 1215-1349.
[2] A paradox (gr. pará=against and doxá=opinion) is a phenomenon which makes you think: This issue can not be true, but it is true! It is a prima facie non-sense sentence, but in fact it is not only possible, but also real and hence (in special circumstances) true. Take for example the sentence: "The last will be the first!"
[3] See Bulson, 2006, p. 35.

four main topics of *Dubliners* in one story and thus anticipates Joyce's move away from writing short stories to novels.[4]

2.2 Content of *The Dead*

The substance of *The Dead* is the gathering of guests at Julia Morkans house to celebrate the annual Christmas party, which the elderly sisters Julia and Kate Morkan organize every year. Among the guests there is Molly Ivors, who does not want to reconcile with the collective oblivion of Irish history and the origins of the Irish language and is therefore very patriotic. A distinguished guest is Bartell D'Arcy, a famous but retired tenor. Mr. Browne is the only Protestant guest at the party. Another guest, Freddy Malins, is an alcoholic and a good friend of Gabriel Conroy, the protagonist of *The Dead*. Further noteworthy characters are Mary Jane Morkhan, a niece of the Morkhan sisters, who gives music lessons, and Lily their maid.

All the guests belong to Dublin's middle class and their conversation revolves around daily things like local incidents, cultural and religious issues as well as political matters.

Shortly after Gabriel and his wife Gretta have arrived at the party, Gabriel talks disparagingly about Lily's marriage prospects.[5] In general he displays a very condescending attitude and behaviour towards people of whose he thinks that they are inferior to him – and these are almost all – except for Miss Ivors. During a heated discussion with Miss Ivors, it becomes clear, that Gabriel's position is much too cosmopolitical for Miss Ivors, whose position is indubitably a nationalist one. The conversation turns into a dispute, which culminates in raptures of Gabriel in the statement: "*I'm sick of my own country, sick of it!*"[6]

At about the midpoint of the narrative, Gabriel holds a speech in which he encourages the audience – even if it is hard – not to let straining thoughts and bad memories from the past overshadow the here and now, but to live in the present and look ahead into the future. This self-satisfying speech is a conceited sermon that addresses the whole group and appears to the reader very dogmatic. At the end of the party, when most of the guests have left the party, the tenor sings a song which affects Gretta in a curious way.

---

[4] See Bulson, 2006, p. 35.
[5] See Joyce, 1914, p. 2173f lines 72-75.
[6] Joyce, 1914, p. 2180 line 402f.

4

After the party, Gabriel and his wife Gretta go to a hotel to stay the night there. Gretta tells Gabriel a story about a young man, Michael Furey, who had sung the same song as the tenor but only because of his love to her. However before Gretta had to leave Dublin the fatally ill Michael Furey visited her and wanted to say goodbye to her. Gretta knew that he suffered from consumption. She dismissed him. Short time after that the young boy died. Now she becomes conscious of that mistake and begins to cry. Gabriel searches for a reason why Gretta is still so affected by this situation and realizes, that for their entire marriage he has been a substitute for a seventeen year old boy, who died once. After this "epiphany" Gabriel feels how much he loves Gretta. The story has an open end and closes with the sentence:

> *"His soul swooned slowly as he heard the snow falling faintly through the universe and faintly falling, like the descent of their last end, upon all the living and the dead."*[7]

2.3 Interpretation of *The Dead*

Let us start with a look at the environment. This is important because the environment is the reason for both, for the unsatisfied and bored lives of the guests at the party and to the failed dreams of the Dubliners in general.[8] The first thing to note is that there is no description of the landscape or region. Joyce does only one thing: He describes things and how they are arranged. Let us take for example his description of the arrangement of food and dishes on the table in the supper-room. Joyce´s description of the arrangement is very detailed and he uses a geometric, technical vocabulary, e.g. "parallel lines of side-dishes"[9], "a solid rectangle of Smyrna figs"[10] and "a pyramid of oranges"[11]. He also uses military expressions like "a round of spiced beef"[12], "between these rival ends ran parallel lines of side-dishes"[13], "two little ministers of jelly"[14], "companion dish"[15], "squads of bottles"[16] and "the colours of their uniforms"[17]. Especially the use of the military vocabulary in relation to the arrangement of the supper-room table is a stylistic way to anthropomorphize lifeless objects. To anthropomorphize inanimate objects means to give them human features. By doing that one

---

[7] Joyce, 1914, p. 2199 lines 1347-1349.
[8] See Müller, 2009, p. 178.
[9] Joyce, 1914, p. 2184 line 592.
[10] Joyce, 1914, p. 2184 line 595f.
[11] Joyce, 1914, p. 2184 line 599.
[12] Joyce, 1914, p. 2184 line 591.
[13] Joyce, 1914, p. 2184 line 591-592.
[14] Joyce, 1914, p. 2184 line 592.
[15] Joyce, 1914, p. 2184 line 595.
[16] Joyce, 1914, p. 2184 line 602.
[17] Joyce, 1914, p. 2184 line 603.

moves inhuman things closer to humans. In reverse, this means that humans lose their special human feature. The stylistic fact of anthropomorphization indicates that Joyce indirectly degrades the people in *The Dead* to objects. At this point we have to take a closer look at the characters in *The Dead*.

The first impression of the characters after reading *The Dead* is quite unspectacular: People in the upper middle class, who gather for a Christmas party. But when we look closer at those characters we will recognize one important thing: Every character has a connection to the past which obstructs him in different ways or he is bound to routine. Mary Jane "gave a pupils´ concert every year in the upper room of the Antient Concert Rooms"[18]. Miss Ivors is bound to the past in the sense that she is not willing to accept the current political and cultural facts. "Freddy Malins always came late"[19] and is bound to the past in virtue due his alcoholism. Gretta has a negative connection to the past because of she dismissed the terminally ill Michael Fury. We can state that the people in *The Dead* have inflexible, rigid patterns and hence can not break traditions (which are at least indicated by the annual gathering to the Christmas party).

To understand the role of the protagonist Gabriel in *The Dead* we will have to look at two things: Firstly, at his character traits and attitudes. Secondly, we have to describe the development of these character traits and attitudes over the whole story.

Gabriel´s character is best described as condescending, arrogant and pseudo intellectual. He is condescending in his behaviour towards Lily and Gretta in making jokes about Lily´s marriage prospects and in exposing Gretta´s dressing habits – in his eyes she takes to long to dress herself.[20] His pseudo intellectuality can best be shown if we split the compound "pseudo intellectuality" up in his elements and try to substantiate our claim of Gabriel´s pseudo intellectuality. Gabriel wants to bee seen as intellectual cosmopolite: His exaggerated speech[21], his writing for the "Daily Express"[22] and his journeys to other countries for vacation "partly to keep in touch with the languages and partly for a change"[23] are examples for his "intellectuality". "Pseudo" becomes this intellectuality, the moment when Gabriel first is intellectually inferior to somebody, namely Miss Ivors. He is inferior to her in the sense that he can not reasonably argue for his position. Miss Ivors shamed him twice, first in devaluing

---

[18] Joyce, 1914, p. 2172 line 22.
[19] Joyce, 1914, p. 2173 line 39.
[20] See Joyce, 1914, p. 2173 lines 45-46 and 74-75.
[21] See Joyce, 1914, pp. 2187-2189 lines 752-830.
[22] See Joyce, 1914, p. 2179 line 347.
[23] Joyce, 1914, p. 2180 line 392f.

the newspaper he writes for and second in attacking that Gabriel is much more concerned about foreign languages than about the Irish. Gabriel can not deal with this situation adequately because he is overtaxed. He is not able to reason the intellectual picture which he wants to suggest to people and therefore he is pseudo intellectual.

Now let us have a look at the development of Gabriel's character traits and attitudes in relation to the whole narrative. At the start Gabriel's view of himself is marked with hubris probably due to his education, gender and his social network. He sees himself in the context that he can (in his mind) charm others, is in possession of abilities (e.g. his intellect) and people (e.g. his wife Gretta) as well as that he can control various situations and people. At about the midpoint of the story – short time before he holds his speech – the flawless picture of himself is attacked by Miss Ivors and hence gets first damage. At the end of *The Dead* Gabriel feels inferior to others, especially to Gretta. This happens when he recognized that he never was in control of Gretta the whole marriage. The reason for this is that Gabriel can not compete with the passion once shared by Gretta and the seventeen-year-old Michael Furey. In this regard, Gabriel loses – by recognizing the enduring feelings of Gretta for Michael Furey – control over Greta he actually never had (except in his mind). In this key scene the dead (Michael Furey) do not only have a connection to the living, the paradox is, that they compete with the living and defeat them! The feelings of Gabriel's wife for a deceased person are much more intense than her feelings towards to her living husband. Viewed in this light, the living are dead and the dead are living. At this point we can state that Gabriel lives in a world in which the living and the dead meet.

After we have investigated these three elements of the storyline we can state the following: The environment degrades the characters into objects. The degraded characters have rigid and inflexible patterns, traditions and behaviour. The protagonist of *The Dead* Gabriel is a condescending, pseudo-intellectual, who wants to be seen as cosmopolite. During the story his character changes from exaggerated hubris to an inferior feeling towards to Gretta. The reason for that is that he recognized that Gretta never loved him so much as the deceased Michael Furey. Now we can try to answer our initial questions.

3. What meaning do the dead have in James Joyce's *The Dead*?

The answer to the question "What connection does the narrative have to the dead?" is that the common view about the connection between the living and the dead – which says that there is no such connection between the living and the dead – is wrong. There is a connection between the realms of the living and the dead and under certain circumstances this connection becomes paradoxical in the sense that was explained above. At this point it is interesting to ask what circumstances must there be for the connection between living and dead to become paradoxical.

The answer to the second question is that the special circumstances which generate the paradoxical connection – accordingly, to the dead being able to compete with and defeat the living – between the living and the dead, are nothing more than the inflexible and rigid attitudes of people (e.g. the belief in the supremacy of tradition in Gabriel's speech[24] and his alleged superiority to Gretta[25]), that interact with the surroundings and cause them to be as rigid and uniform (e.g. the dishes and the food on the table and Joyce's geometric and military vocabulary to describe it) as the attitudes of the people themselves are. You can see the interaction between the people and their surroundings in a detailed sense:

> *"On the closed square piano a pudding in a huge yellow dish lay in waiting and behind it were three squads of bottles of stout and ale and minerals, drawn up according to the colours of their uniforms, the first two black, with brown and red labels, the third and smallest squad white, with transverse green sashes"*.[26]

Or you can see the interaction in a broader sense, when you generally look at Dublin and see that Dublin was on the one hand strictly Catholic and at the zenith of its industrialisation, but on the other hand the Dubliners suffered – not at least because of Catholicism and industrialisation – from alcoholism, unemployment and poverty.[27] The crucial point in the interpretation of the paradoxical connection between the living and the dead depends less on the fact of whether to one is alive or dead, but more on the fact of what you do or have done. People including Gabriel live lethargic lives and in patterns they never change or scrutinize. They are confident with their situation because they do not realize that their lives are only lives in the sense of vegetation and hence their "lives" are closer to what is called death than

---

[24] See Joyce, 1914, pp. 2187-2189 lines 752-830.
[25] See Joyce, 1914, p. 2175 line 135-136.
[26] Joyce, 1914, p. 2184 lines 601-605.
[27] See Schneider, 1997, pp. 17-19.

to what is called life. In contrast the actual dead who did not have such lethargic, catatonic lives, but lives which were closer to the term "life" in the common sense, are more alive than dead, because either their deeds in the past still affect something in the present or the living people keep them alive by never forgetting them. Gabriel originally was convinced of the fact that there is a division between the past of the dead and the present of the living. Michael Furey is dead, but because of Gretta´s passionate memories alive. Gabriel is indeed alive, but without emotions. At the end of *The Dead* Gabriel´s epiphany is that his originally view about the division between the living and the dead is wrong.

The paradoxical connection between the living and the dead has its reason and causation in "living" people, who do not live their lives by reflecting and realizing who they are. By doing so, they would recognize, that humans are alive because of the feelings which constitute their "selves". Humans have emotions and emotions are one of the primary differences between the living and the dead: The Dead do not have emotions. The living have emotions and the more they become conscious of their emotions and the more they show and live their emotions, the more alive they are.

To sum up, the moral conclusion of *The Dead* which Joyce wants the reader to have is that those who feel emotions are true to themselves and those who feel not are not. One never should overestimate oneself and underestimate others. Without emotions you are just like Gabriel: You are more joining the realm of the dead than the realm of the living.

4. Literature

Primary Sources:

Joyce, James (1914): *The Dead*, in: Dubliners p. 2172-2199.

Secondary Sources:

Bulson, Eric (2006): *The Cambridge Introduction to James Joyce*, Cambridge University Press 2006.

Müller, Timo (2009): *The Self as Object in Modernist Fiction – James, Joyce, Hemingway* text&theorie band 11 herausgegeben von Martin Middeke und Hubert Zapf, Köngshausen & Neumann Würzburg 2009.

Schneider, Ulrich (1997): *James Joyce – Studien zu Dubliners und Ulysses*, Erlanger Forschungen Reihe A – Geisteswissenschaften – Band 78 herausgegeben von Eberhard Kreutzer, Arno Löffler und Dieter Petzold Erlangen 1997.

Further Reading:

Campbell, Matthew (2009): *Nineteenth-century lyric nationalism*, in: James Joyce in Context, edited by John McCourt, Cambridge University Press 2009 p. 184-194.

Eide, Marian (2009): *Gender and sexuality*, in: James Joyce in Context, edited by John McCourt, Cambridge University Press 2009 p. 76-87.

Latham, Sean (2009): *Twenty-first-century critical contexts*, in: James Joyce in Context, edited by John McCourt, Cambridge University Press 2009 p. 148-160.

Latham, Sean (2010): *James Joyce*, Irish Academic Press 2010.

Leonard, Garry (1990): *Dubliners*, in: The Cambridge Companion to James Joyce edited by Derek Attridge, Cambridge University Press 2004 p. 87-102.

Nash, John (2009): *Genre, place and value: Joyce's reception, 1904-1941*, in: James Joyce in Context, edited by John McCourt, Cambridge University Press 2009 p. 41-51.

O'Rourke, Fran (2009): *Philosophy*, in: James Joyce in Context, edited by John McCourt, Cambridge University Press 2009 p. 320-331.

Temple Herr, Cheryl (2009): *Being in Joyce's world*, in: James Joyce in Context, edited by John McCourt, Cambridge University Press 2009 p. 163-172.